A to Z Mindfulness

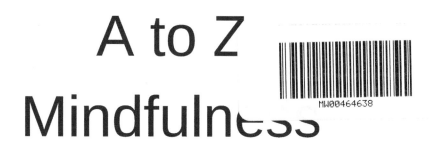

A Coping Skills Coloring Book for Kids

Written by Leanne Richter, LMFT and Shauna Havlina, LMFT
Illustrations by: Ignacio Guerrero Hernandez
Cover Design and Layout: Jeffrey Vallis

Copyright © 2017 by Leanne Richter and Shauna Havlina

All rights reserved. No part of this publication may be reproduced, distributed, or transmitted in any form or by any means, including photocopying, recording, or other electronic or mechanical methods, without the prior written permission of the publisher, except in the case of brief quotations embodied in critical reviews and certain other noncommercial uses permitted by copyright law. For permission requests, email leannerichtermft@gmail.com

Ordering Information:
Quantity sales. Special discounts are available on quantity purchases by corporations, associations, and others. For details, contact the authors at leannerichtermft@gmail.com

Printed in the United States of America

This coloring book is meant to be a tool to help children use mindfulness skills as a way to cope with stress, anxiety, and anger. Children can use it on their own: coloring the pictures, drawing, and practicing the skills on each page. Or, they can use it with an adult who cares about them. Parents, teachers, and counselors can guide them to practice the skill listed on each page. This is a great way to start a conversation about mindfulness. Children may need extra coaching or explanations about the skills included.

Each page also includes an affirmation to improve confidence, positive self talk, and emotional expression. These affirmations can be repeated throughout the day. Parents can use them as reminders when a child is feeling overwhelmed by a big emotion or is in need of encouragement.

We hope that this can be a fun and useful way to teach the children in your life about mindfulness and coping with stressors!

A is for Art

Draw something in the box below that makes you happy.

Practice Saying

Today is going to be a good day

B is for Breathe

Take three deep breaths in your nose and slowly out your mouth. Now, pretend you are blowing bubbles! See how far you can get the bubbles to go.

Practice Saying

With every breath I quiet my mind

C is for Count to 100

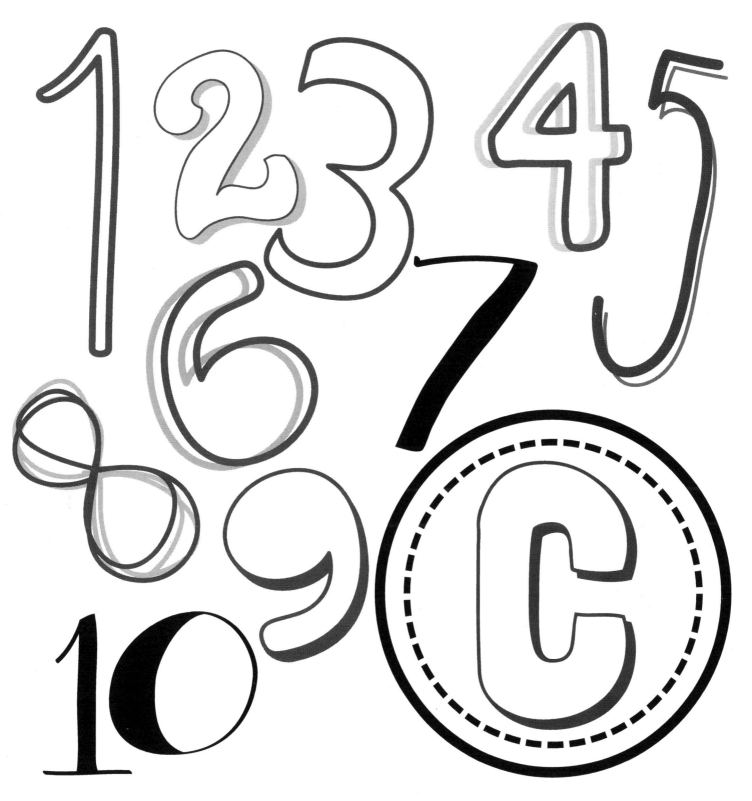

Practice Saying

I can solve problems

D is for Draw

Draw 3 things that you see in the room around you.

E is for
Eat a Snack

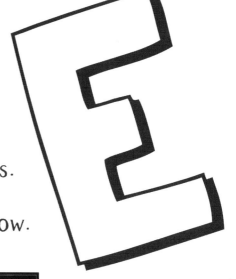

Pay attention to how the food tastes.

Describe how it tastes in the box below.

Practice Saying

My body is a gift that I am thankful for

F is for Focus

Close your eyes and take three deep breaths. Pay extra special attention to what you can hear. Draw a picture of one of the things you hear.

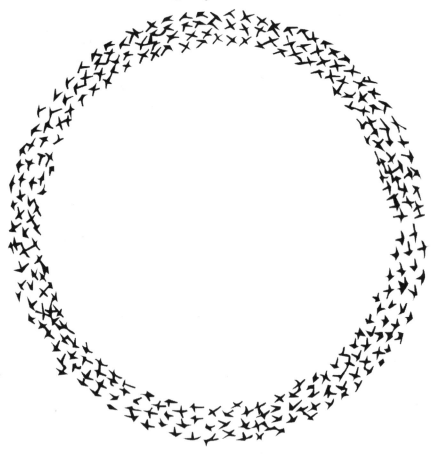

G is for Gratitude

Draw a picture of something you

are thankful for.

Practice Saying

I am thankful for people who love me

H is for Heartbeat

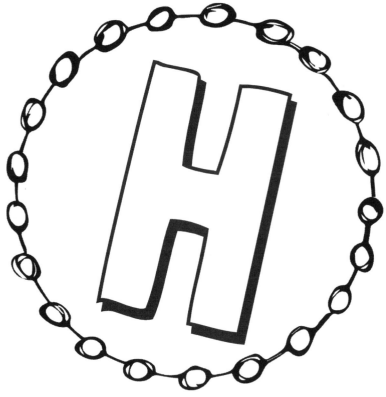

Place your hand over your heart, take three deep breaths and pay attention to what your heart beat feels like.

Practice Saying

I have a strong body than can do many things

I is for Imagine

Imagine you are in a safe and peaceful place. What does it look like? Feel like? Smell like? Draw a picture of your safe place.

Practice Saying

I am in charge of my thoughts

J is for Jump

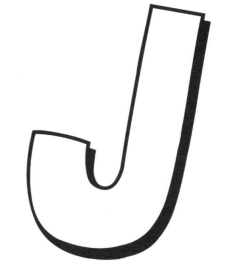

Jump up and down while you
count to 20. Write down how
you felt before the jump and
then after.

Practice Saying

I am in charge of my body

K is for Kindness

Name 3 things you like about yourself.

K

1

2

3

I like myself just as I am

L is for Let it Go

Think of something you are worried about. Now, picture that thing getting tied to a balloon and floating away.

Practice Saying

I am me, and I am okay!

M is for Music

Listen to your favorite song or sing a

song as loud as you can!

Practice Saying

I have lots of gifts and talents

N is for...

Name one thing you are feeling right now. What does that feeling look like? Draw it below.

O is for Open your eyes

Look all around you. What do you see?

Practice Saying

I trust myself to make good choices

P is for Pretend

Pretend you are on a surf board riding the waves.

Practice Saying

Even when I feel frustrated, I won't give up

Q is for
Quiet your mind

Find a comfortable spot and sit quietly with your eyes closed. Take three deep breath and imagine you are watching your thoughts float away.

Practice Saying

I have a wise and creative mind

R is for Run

Run in place while you count to 10. Describe how your body feels after you have been running.

Practice Saying

I can keep trying, even when things are difficult

S is for Stretch

Stand up and Stretch your arms high over your head.

Practice Saying

I am the best at being myself

T is for Tapping

Use your hands to tap your head, tap your arms, tap your tummy.

It's brave to try new things

U is for UP!

Stretch your hands **UP** to the sky as high as you can and wiggle your fingers.

Practice Saying

I can breathe out anger and breathe in joy

V is for visualize

Visualize your favorite place in the whole world. Draw a picture of your favorite place.

Practice Saying

I am good, even when I make mistakes

W is for Walk

Go for a walk.

Notice how your body feels while you are walking.

Practice Saying

Today I chose to love and accept myself

X is for X-ray Vision

Close your eyes and image you can see inside your body. Picture your muscles, bones, heart, and lungs.

Today I choose to be kind

Y is for Yoga

Practice doing Triangle Pose. Hop your feet open and turn your right toes out and your left toes slightly in; then bend to your side and place your right hand on your shin or the ground as you look up to your left hand. Come up to a standing position and repeat on other side.

Practice Saying

It is good to learn new things

Z is for Zzzzz

Lay flat on your back and close your eyes. Picture your body sinking into the floor. Notice what thoughts come into your mind and write them below.

Practice Saying

I am always doing the best that I can

Name These Feelings

Practice Saying

It's okay to ask for help when I need it

91405808R00018

Made in the USA
Middletown, DE
30 September 2018